Who Was
Sojourner Truth?

by Yona Zeldis McDonough
illustrated by Jim Eldridge

Grosset & Dunlap
An Imprint of Penguin Random House

For Jane O'Connor—one in a million!—YZM

GROSSET & DUNLAP
Penguin Young Readers Group
An Imprint of Penguin Random House LLC

Text copyright © 2015 by Yona Zeldis McDonough. Illustrations copyright © 2015 by Penguin Random House LLC. All rights reserved. Published by Grosset & Dunlap, an imprint of Penguin Random House LLC, 345 Hudson Street, New York, New York 10014. Who HQ™ and all related logos are trademarks owned by Penguin Random House LLC. GROSSET & DUNLAP is a trademark of Penguin Random House LLC. Printed in the USA.

Library of Congress Cataloging-in-Publication Data is available.

ISBN 978-0-448-48678-9   10 9 8 7 6 5 4

Contents

Who Was
Sojourner Truth?

JUNE 1, 1843

The tall woman walked down to the ferry in
New York City, paid the fare, and got on.

Although the woman was black and had been born a slave, she was now free to come and go as she pleased. When the ride ended, she got off the ferry and began to walk. Soon, the hustle and bustle of the city was far behind her. After a while, she grew thirsty and stopped at a farm to ask for a drink. The woman who gave it to her asked her name. The tall woman thought about this. The only full name she had was a slave name, given to her by her master. She did not want that name anymore. She was starting a new life. She was going to be doing a lot of traveling. And she was going to spread the word of God.

So, right then and there she gave herself a new name. She decided to call herself Sojourner Truth, and this is her story.

Chapter 1
Early Days

Sometime around 1797, a baby girl was born to slaves named James and Betsey. She was called Isabella. Her nickname was Belle. Because her parents were slaves, Isabella was a slave, too.

This meant that they belonged to someone. They were not free. Their master was a white man named Johannes Hardenbergh. Since Mr. Hardenbergh was from Holland, he spoke Dutch. That was the language Belle grew up speaking, too.

James and Betsey worked very hard on Mr. Hardenbergh's farm. He did not pay them. They could not leave. They had to do whatever he wanted. It was a harsh and terrible life. They had many children—maybe as many as twelve. Almost all of them were sold by Mr. Hardenbergh. Betsey and James never saw these children again.

The farm Belle and her parents lived on was in Swartekill, New York. Many people think that slavery only existed in Southern states like Virginia, Louisiana, Georgia, Alabama, and Mississippi. But back in the 1700s, slavery was legal in many Northern states, too.

When Belle was about three, Johannes Hardenbergh died. His son Charles inherited all his property. This meant Charles owned his father's house, his land, his horses, and his cows. And his father's slaves.

Charles took the slaves and the animals to his home. He had no room for these people, so they

had to live in the cellar. The cellar was cold, dark, and damp. It was smelly and crowded, too— twelve slaves lived there. Belle's bed was a wooden board.

Not long after her family moved to the cellar, Belle had a surprise. It was a new baby brother. His name was Peter.

Betsey was happy about her son. But Betsey also worried. Her other children had been sold. Belle and Peter might be sold, too. Betsey hoped that God would protect them. As Betsey's children grew, she told them about God, who was in heaven. Whenever they were scared or sad, they could always ask God for help.

In 1806, Charles Hardenbergh died. Belle was about nine. What would happen to her family now? Shortly after the funeral, Charles's property was sold off. By this time, Belle's father, James, could no longer do much work. His back was bent and stooped. He also had arthritis, a disease that crippled his hands and legs.

Slaves like James were hard to sell. Often they ended up getting "turned out" by their masters. This meant that they were free. But they were not given a place to live or any money to live on. They were old and often sick, so they could not take care of themselves. As a result, these slaves often died. Along with James, Betsey was turned out. Where would they go? They begged to stay. The Hardenbergh family agreed. They could remain in the cellar.

Belle and Peter were young and able to work hard. Healthy slaves, especially boys, were worth a lot of money. At a slave auction, they both were sold. Peter was sold first.

He went to a man who did not live close by. Belle was so sad. But she remembered what her mother had said about God. He would protect her. So Belle silently repeated a prayer she knew.

After Peter was sold and led away, it was Belle's turn on the block. The auctioneer called out her name and told the buyers about her. She did not speak English, only Dutch, so she could not understand what he said. But she got the idea loud and clear.

At first there were no buyers. Then the auctioneer added a flock of sheep. Finally a man named John Neely bought her for one hundred dollars.

SLAVE AUCTIONS

WHEN SLAVES FROM AFRICA WERE BROUGHT TO THE UNITED STATES, THEY WERE SOLD AT AUCTION. HELD IN PENS, THEIR SKIN WAS SMEARED WITH GREASE OR TAR TO MAKE IT LOOK HEALTHY. THEY WERE BRANDED LIKE CATTLE. BUYERS FORCED THEIR MOUTHS OPEN TO SEE IF THEY HAD GOOD TEETH, AND TESTED THEIR MUSCLES FOR STRENGTH. THE BIGGEST, STRONGEST-LOOKING SLAVES WERE BOUGHT FIRST BECAUSE IT WAS THOUGHT THEY COULD WORK THE HARDEST. FAMILIES WERE SPLIT UP, AND NEVER SAW EACH OTHER AGAIN.

IN A "GRAB AND GO" AUCTION, THE BUYER GAVE THE SLAVE TRADER A SET AMOUNT OF MONEY. A DRUMROLL SOUNDED AND THE SLAVE PEN OPENED. THE BUYER RUSHED IN AND GRABBED THE SLAVE OR SLAVES THAT HE WANTED. IN A "HIGHEST BIDDER" AUCTION, SLAVES WERE SHOWN ONE AT A TIME. IF MORE THAN ONE BUYER WANTED A SLAVE, THE BUYERS WOULD BID. THE BUYER WHO BID THE MOST MONEY WON.

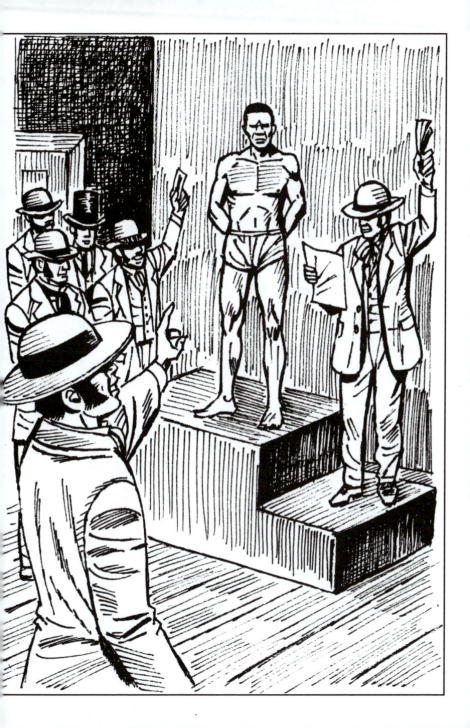

Mr. Neely thought he got a good deal. But his wife did not think so. The Neelys were from England. They spoke English, not Dutch. They lived near Kingston, New York, and ran a store. The store was not doing well. Most of the people who lived nearby were Dutch. They did not trust the English owners, so they did not shop at the store. Mrs. Neely took out her anger at the Dutch settlers on Belle.

Belle was the only slave owned by the Neelys. They made her work inside the house, cleaning and cooking.

Belle found her new life hard. She missed her parents, and since she did not speak English, she did not understand what was said to her. She tried her best to learn English, but Mrs. Neely was not a good teacher. When Belle got a word wrong, Mrs. Neely slapped her.

One Sunday morning, Mrs. Neely was so mad, she sent Belle out to the barn. Mr. Neely was waiting there. He beat her so badly that she fainted. Belle had never been beaten before. She told herself she would work extra hard to keep from being beaten again.

Not too long after this, her father came to
visit. He saw that Belle had no shoes. Her thin
clothes were no protection against the winter cold.
James was sick and old. Yet he saw Belle's suffering
and knew he had to help her. Since he had been
turned out, he was no longer a slave, but he didn't
have the money to buy Belle and set her free.
Maybe he could help another way.

James got Martin Schryver to buy Belle.
Schryver was a fisherman. He also had a farm and

a tavern. He and his wife were not educated people. But they were not cruel. And they spoke both Dutch and English. This made life easier for Belle, and she was able to learn English more easily now, too.

For the next eighteen months, Belle lived with the Schryvers. She grew tall and strong like her father had once been. All day long she worked. When the fishing boats came in, she helped unload them. In the fields, she planted corn—and hoed it, too. She did errands and worked at the tavern.

Unlike her other masters, the Schryvers gave her enough food, warm clothes, and a decent place to live. But kind as her new masters were, they did not allow Belle to go to school. Slaves were forbidden from learning to read and write. Those who disobeyed were severely punished.

It was while Belle was at the Schryvers that she got terrible news. Her mother had died. Now her family would never be reunited. And what would happen to her father? He could not manage on his own. Belle was right to worry. Her father died not long after her mother. With her brother far away, Belle was now alone in the world. Once again she thought of her mother's words. God was watching her. God cared about her. She would never be alone.

One day, a man came into the tavern. He saw how strong Belle was and offered to buy her for three hundred dollars. That was three times as much as the Schryvers had paid for her.

Even though the Schryvers had agreed to buy
Belle, now they sold her. She went to New Paltz
with her new master, John Dumont. She did not
know what he would be like. But she would soon
find out.

Chapter 2
Freedom Ahead

In 1810, John Dumont wrote in his record book that Belle was "about thirteen" but that she stood "nearly six feet tall." He bragged about her. He said she could do more work than his strongest male slaves. But his wife did not like her. She told the white maids that they should "lord it over" poor Belle. That meant they could give Belle a hard time. In fact, Mrs. Dumont wanted them to "grind her down."

One time, when Belle boiled potatoes, Mrs. Dumont scolded her. She said the water in the pot was dirty. The next day, Belle scrubbed the potatoes extra hard. They were clean before she put them in water to boil. But later when Mrs. Dumont looked in the pot, the water was

dirty. Mrs. Dumont was very angry. Belle didn't
understand how this had happened.

Luckily, Belle had a friend in the house. Gertrude, Mrs. Dumont's ten-year-old daughter, liked her. Gertrude thought that Katie, one of the maids, was the problem. So she hatched a plan. Belle set the potatoes to boil. Then she went to milk the cow. Gertrude hid in the kitchen. She saw Katie come in and sprinkle ashes in the pot. Gertrude jumped out of her hiding place. She told her parents what Katie had done. Belle was not blamed anymore.

Despite Gertrude's kindness, Belle was lonely
at the Dumonts'. Then she met Robert. He was
a slave, too. She first saw him at a feast that
came fifty days after Easter. There was dancing,
singing, and food. Robert began visiting Belle.
They fell in love.

Mr. Catlin, Robert's master, did not like this. He wanted Robert to marry one of his own slaves. That way, any children born would belong to Mr. Catlin, too. If Robert and Belle had children, they would belong to Mr. Dumont. Robert did not obey his master. He continued to visit Belle in secret. When Mr. Catlin caught him, he beat him.

Belle begged Mr. Dumont to do something.
Although it was highly unusual, Mr. Dumont told
Mr. Catlin to stop. He ordered Mr. Catlin off his
property. Then he followed him home to make
sure he did not kill Robert. But Mr. Catlin did
not plan to kill Robert. He beat him to make him
obey. And it worked. Robert did not visit Belle
anymore. He married the woman his master had
chosen.

Mr. Dumont decided Belle needed a husband.
He picked one of his own field slaves named
Thomas. Belle wanted to be married by a
preacher, and Mr. Dumont agreed. Belle and
Thomas were married around 1817. Belle was
about twenty years old.

Belle and Tom grew to care for each other.
Tom had been married before. After his first wife

was sold, he had run away to find her. He loved her very much. Tom never did find her because slave catchers found *him*. He was sent back to the Dumonts', where he was beaten. His scars made Belle weep. Tom was a good man.

One year after they married, Belle and Tom had a daughter, Diana. Over the next ten years, they would have four more children: Elizabeth, Hannah, Peter, and Sophia.

SLAVE CATCHERS

IN 1857, THERE WAS A LANDMARK COURT CASE INVOLVING A MAN NAMED DRED SCOTT. HE WAS A SLAVE WHO HAD ESCAPED FROM HIS MASTER AND LIVED IN A FREE STATE FOR MANY YEARS. BUT THE COURT DECIDED THAT DIDN'T MEAN HE WAS FREE. HE WAS STILL A SLAVE AND HAD TO RETURN TO HIS MASTER. AS A RESULT OF THE DECISION, THERE WAS NOW MONEY TO BE MADE IN CATCHING ESCAPED SLAVES AND RETURNING THEM TO THEIR OWNERS. SLAVE CATCHERS WERE THE PEOPLE WHO HUNTED DOWN THE RUNAWAY SLAVES. THEY WERE PAID FOR EVERY SLAVE THEY CAUGHT. THE RETURNED SLAVES WERE BRUTALLY PUNISHED WITH BEATINGS AND WHIPPINGS.

Wonderful news arrived in 1817! A new law was passed in New York State. All slaves born before July 4, 1799, had to be freed by July 4, 1827. This meant Belle and her husband would be set free in ten years. (Since their children had been born after 1799, they would not be free until the boys were twenty-eight and the girls were twenty-five.) John Dumont even promised that he would free Belle and Tom in 1826, a year earlier than the law called for. They could live in a cabin on his land.

In exchange for her early freedom, Belle agreed to work even longer hours than usual. She worked in the fields planting crops. She worked in the house washing, cooking, and cleaning. She spun big piles of wool into yarn for knitting.

Then she hurt her hand on a scythe, which is a sharp hand tool used to cut grass or reap crops. The wound did not heal. Still, she kept her part of the bargain. But when freedom day came, Mr. Dumont did not honor his promise. He said Belle could not have done much extra work with a wounded hand. The deal was off.

Belle was furious. Tom told her not to be upset—they would be freed the next year. But Belle was not waiting. She woke up early and put her few belongings in a pillowcase. She knew she could not take all her children with her, so she left the four eldest with Tom and took only the baby, Sophia.

Then she snuck away from Mr. Dumont's farm.

Belle went to a white family named the Van Wageners. She had learned of them through Levi Rowe, a Quaker who lived down the road. The Van Wageners were abolitionists. That meant they thought slavery was wrong. They would do whatever they could to help runaway slaves. The Van Wageners let Belle and her baby stay with them. She would work for them, but they would not own her. She could leave anytime she wanted.

QUAKERS

THE QUAKERS, ALSO CALLED FRIENDS, ARE A CHRISTIAN GROUP STARTED IN ENGLAND IN THE MID-1600S. QUAKERS BELIEVE THAT PEOPLE DO NOT NEED MINISTERS TO COMMUNICATE WITH GOD. INSTEAD, A PERSON CAN SPEAK DIRECTLY TO GOD. THE QUAKERS WHO LIVED IN NINETEENTH-CENTURY AMERICA DRESSED IN PLAIN AND SIMPLE CLOTHES. THEY WERE AGAINST ALL FORMS OF VIOLENCE AND REFUSED TO FIGHT IN ANY WARS. THEY WERE ALSO ABOLITIONISTS AND RISKED THEIR LIVES BY HELPING MANY SLAVES ESCAPE TO FREEDOM.

Hours later, John Dumont found Belle in her
new home. He wanted her back, but she refused
to go. The Van Wageners paid him twenty dollars
to free her a year early. They paid five dollars
for Sophia. Belle and her child were free at last.
But Belle's happiness was short-lived. She found
out her son, Peter, had been sold to slave owners in
Alabama. She would never see him again.

Belle could not accept this. From her Quaker
friends Belle learned that selling Peter to a

Southern state was against the law. In New York, you could not sell slaves out of state. So the law was on Belle's side. Later Belle remembered thinking, "I was sure God would help me to get him. Why, I felt so tall within—I felt as if the power of a nation was with me."

Belle's Quaker friends told her what to do. They sent her to Poppletown, New York. It was close to the county seat in Kingston. The Quaker couple had friends there who would let her stay in their house. Belle walked to Poppletown.

It took Belle almost all day to get there. She had never walked so far all by herself, and when she finally got there, she was very tired. Her hosts offered her food and a bed for the night.

Years later, Belle wrote that she had never slept in such a "nice, high, clean, white, beautiful bed." She was too scared to get in, so she crawled under it instead. Then she worried she might offend her hosts, so she crawled out and slept in the beautiful bed.

The next day she went to the courthouse.
There, she filed a complaint against the man who
sold Peter out of state. His name was Solomon
Gedney. The judge agreed with Belle. The sale
was against the law. Mr. Gedney could not believe
there was all this fuss over a
slave. It took many months,
but Peter was returned to
his mother. (Since
Gedney had
broken the law
in selling Peter,
Peter was now
free.) Belle
had won. She
was one of
the first black
women in the
country to win
a case like this.

Belle and Peter stayed and worked for the Van Wageners in Kingston. Sophia, who was about two years old, went to live at the Dumonts' with her sisters Diana, Hannah, and Elizabeth. Belle's husband, Tom, was freed on July 4, 1828, but he stayed in New Paltz. Tom's health was not good, making it hard for him and Belle to live together. He died by the end of the year. All he got was a little taste of freedom.

Life with the Van Wageners was comfortable. Belle was able to visit her daughters. She and Peter joined a Methodist church.

There she met a schoolteacher from New York City named Miss Geer. Miss Geer liked Belle and thought Peter was very bright. She encouraged Belle to move to New York City. There were plenty of jobs there. Best of all, there were schools for black children.

Belle talked it over with her daughters and

they thought it was a good idea. They promised
to take care of Sophia. So Belle decided to leave.
She made this decision by herself. She did not have
to ask a master's permission. At the end of the
summer of 1829, Belle and Peter took a boat down
the Hudson River. They were on their way to New
York City. A new life was waiting for them.

Chapter 3
The Big City

In 1829, almost two hundred thousand people
lived in New York City. Belle had never seen such

crowds. But she soon learned her way around. She went to work as a servant for a family named Whiting, and then another called Gatfield. Later, she worked for a family who owned a newspaper. Peter went to school.

Belle joined the Zion Church, which would later be called the Mother Zion African Methodist Episcopal Church. The church had been founded in 1796. The bishop had even ordained a woman, Jarena Lee. Belle was inspired by her example. It meant Belle could be a minister, too. She liked the church

JARENA LEE

very much and found peace and comfort there.

One Sunday after services, Belle was approached
by a man and a woman. They seemed to know
her. It turned out they were her sister Sophia and
brother Michael. They had not seen each other in
so many years! Sophia and Michael were free now,
too. They had heard she was in New York City
and worshipped at Zion Church, so they came to
find her. The three siblings were overjoyed to be
together.

Belle began helping out at the church. First she joined a group that brought church teachings to poor people. But Belle thought people needed more than hymns and sermons. The people needed food, clothing, and a decent place to live, too. So she began to help out at a shelter for homeless women.

She also began to lead prayers and songs at her church. People were moved by her strong voice and powerful words. The church held prayer meetings throughout the city. Belle joined these, too. People came just to hear her preach. Her faith in God gave others faith as well.

But while Belle was doing fine in her new life, Peter was not. He dropped out of school. He could not hold a job. He hung around with older boys who encouraged him to steal, and he got caught—more than once. Belle tried to help him, but it was not easy. He would not listen to her. He kept getting into trouble. Finally, she persuaded him to become a sailor. She thought the rules would be good for him.

Peter sailed off on a ship called the *Zone of Nantucket* in 1839. Belle missed him. She wanted to write to him, but she did not know how. So Belle had other people write letters for her.

She told them what to say. Peter only answered a few, and then he stopped writing back altogether. She never heard from him again. But she believed God was protecting him.

Meanwhile, Belle was thinking about her own life. Things were good. She had a place to live and a job. She could feed and clothe herself. She had her church and her friends. But it was not enough—she wanted more. Yet she did not know what it was she wanted.

Belle was deep in prayer when she heard a voice in her head saying, *Go east*. What did that mean? Belle believed the words came directly from God. He was giving her directions. He was guiding her. Other people might think she was crazy, but she did not care. God had spoken. She would listen to those words.

Chapter 4
A New Name, a New Calling

Belle gave notice. That meant she was quitting her job. The next morning, June 1, 1843, she walked down to the ferry and paid two shillings, which was about twenty-five cents, to get on.

She was on her way east—to Connecticut. All she carried was a pillowcase. By the time evening came, she was far outside the city. She stopped at the home of a Quaker to ask for water. The woman asked her name. She said her name was Sojourner. A *sojourner* is a traveler, someone who never stays in one place very long. And that's what Sojourner planned to do. She was setting out to be a traveling preacher.

The woman asked her second name. Sojourner hesitated. She had never had a second name. She had always been Hardenbergh's Belle. Or Dumont's Belle. She was called by the name of her owners. These were slave names. What was *her* name?

Then it came to her. She was devoting herself to God's word. And God's word was true. She told the woman her second name was Truth. Her new name fit her new life: Sojourner Truth.

Sojourner was forty-six when she took her new name and started her new life. She spent the summer and fall preaching in New York, Connecticut, and Massachusetts. People came to hear her at churches and at outdoor meetings.

By the winter of 1843, she was tired. She needed to rest. She joined a new community in western Massachusetts. It was called the Northampton Association of Education and Industry.

WILLIAM LLOYD GARRISON

Blacks and whites lived and worked together in the Association. They ran a silk factory and lived on the money made from selling silk. Many were abolitionists. Sometimes they invited famous speakers to give talks. One was William Lloyd Garrison. Another was Frederick Douglass. Like Sojourner Truth, Douglass had been a slave. He spoke and wrote about his experiences.

FREDERICK DOUGLASS (1818–1895)

FREDERICK DOUGLASS WAS BORN A SLAVE IN MARYLAND. IN 1838, HE ESCAPED NORTH BY PRETENDING TO BE A SAILOR. HE SETTLED IN MASSACHUSETTS, JOINED THE ABOLITIONIST MOVEMENT, AND BECAME A POWERFUL SPEAKER AND WRITER. HE WROTE THREE AUTOBIOGRAPHIES, PUBLISHED A NEWSPAPER, AND SUPPORTED WOMEN'S RIGHTS. HE BECAME A TRUSTED ADVISER TO PRESIDENT ABRAHAM LINCOLN.

Sojourner also heard speakers talk about
women's rights. In the 1840s, women could not
vote or own property. They could not pass laws
or act as leaders. Many people thought being a
wife and mother was the only role for a woman.
Very few paying jobs were open to them. Women's

rights supporters had different ideas. They
believed women and men should be equal under
the law.

In 1846, the Northampton Association ran
out of money and closed. Sojourner was sad. She
went back to working for white people. But she

was fired up by all the speakers she had met. She had become friendly with Olive Gilbert, who was also a member of the Northampton Association and an early supporter of women's rights. Olive told Sojourner about the first Women's Rights Convention in Seneca Falls, New York. Sojourner began to think about women's rights and her life as a former slave.

Frederick Douglass had written about his life in slavery. Now Olive encouraged Sojourner to do

the same. Sojourner still did not know how to write. But she had dictated letters to Peter, so Sojourner dictated her life story to Olive. William Lloyd Garrison printed it. He also wrote an introduction. *Narrative of Sojourner Truth: A Northern Slave* was published in 1850.

That same year, Sojourner paid to have a small house built in Northampton. It cost three hundred dollars. She borrowed the money. She would repay it with money from the sales of her book. This house would give her something she had never had before: peace and security.

SENECA FALLS CONVENTION

HELD IN SENECA FALLS, NEW YORK, ON JULY 19–20, 1848, THE CONVENTION WAS THE FIRST LARGE GATHERING ON WOMEN'S RIGHTS. OVER THREE HUNDRED PEOPLE ATTENDED. MANY IMPORTANT SPEAKERS GAVE TALKS, AND THE CHANGING ROLE OF WOMEN IN SOCIETY WAS HOTLY DISCUSSED.

THE SENECA FALLS CONVENTION IS CONSIDERED TO BE THE BEGINNING OF THE WOMEN'S RIGHTS MOVEMENT. THE CONVENTION WAS AN ANNUAL EVENT HELD IN VARIOUS LOCATIONS UNTIL THE OUTBREAK OF THE CIVIL WAR IN 1861.

Chapter 5
"Ain't I a Woman?"

Sojourner's book did not sell well. People did not know her name yet. She was not as famous as Frederick Douglass. Sojourner kept going to abolitionist meetings and tried to sell her books after the meetings.

At one meeting in late 1850, Sojourner was invited to speak. This was a surprise. She had not known she would be asked. But she did not want to say no. She began with a hymn she had written. Then she told her story. She talked about her life as a slave. She spoke of her father's death. Of being beaten. Of losing Peter. When she was done, everyone cheered. Many people cried. She sold lots of books that night and was able to set aside money to help pay for her house. After that meeting, she decided she would go on more speaking tours. She could sell her books after her speeches. That was a good way to earn a living.

In 1851, Sojourner spoke at a women's rights convention in Akron, Ohio. Hundreds of people were there. Some supported women's rights. But many did not. Speakers got up and gave their speeches. Would Sojourner be one of them? It was not certain. Some women's rights supporters did not want her to speak. They did not want the abolitionist issue and the women's rights issue to get mixed up. They argued it was better to keep the two issues separate. But in the end, Sojourner got up to give a speech.

Sojourner was calm when she spoke. Her voice was deep and powerful. Her words made her audience sit up and listen. Here is some of what she said:

> I have plowed and planted and gathered into barns, and no man could head me— and ain't I a woman? I could work as much and eat as much as a man (when I could get it) and bear the lash as well—and ain't I a woman? I have borne . . . children and seen all sold off into slavery, and when I cried out with a mother's grief, none but Jesus heard me—and ain't I a woman?

At first, the crowd was silent. Then there was cheering and applause. It was a great moment for

Sojourner. She had stood up and spoken her truth:
All black people and all women deserved the same
rights as white men. People of good conscience
had to see this.

After this speech, Sojourner's fame grew. People came to meet her. Journalists wrote about her. Even people who did not agree with her respected her. She borrowed a horse and buggy and piled it high with six hundred copies of her book.

Sojourner rode through Ohio and Indiana, making speeches about women's rights and ending slavery. Often, she let her horse choose the direction. She did not worry about food, clothes, or where she would stay. She had her faith. It kept her strong. God would provide.

Chapter 6
War!

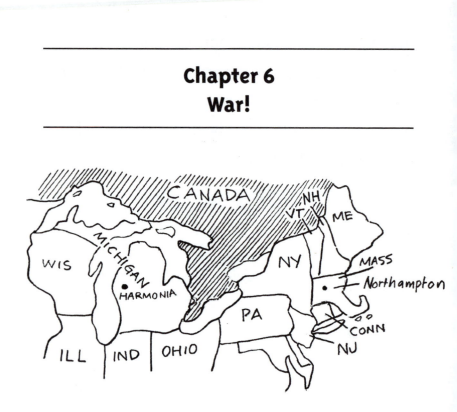

In 1857, when she was sixty years old,
Sojourner sold her house in Northampton,
Massachusetts. She moved to a small community
in Michigan called Harmonia, near Battle Creek.
Like the Northampton Association, Harmonia

was a place where blacks and whites lived side by side. Blacks were treated equally.

Many abolitionists lived in the area, too. They were proud to have Sojourner as a neighbor. And she was happy to be living among kindhearted, educated people who were free from prejudice. Sojourner wanted to spend time with her daughters Diana and Elizabeth and their sons, James Caldwell and Samuel Banks, who were all living nearby.

Sammy was her favorite. He was Elizabeth's son. He did chores for Sojourner. He helped her around the house. When he learned to read, he read the Bible to her. He kept her company.

Maybe Sammy reminded her of Peter, the son who sailed away. Sammy and his grandmother became very close.

Meanwhile, the question of slavery was tearing the United States apart. By this time slavery had been outlawed in all the Northern states. Many in

FREE STATES   SLAVE STATES

the North thought slavery should end everywhere in the country. But the Southern states still clung to their slaves. Rich Southerners had large farms and needed free labor to plant and harvest crops such as cotton, rice, and tobacco. Although the government passed different laws to deal with the problem and keep the country whole, it wasn't working.

Finally, in 1861, eleven Southern states broke away and formed their own country: the Confederate States of America. The Civil War started. Northern soldiers fought against Southern soldiers.

One of Sojourner's grandsons, James Caldwell, signed up with the Northern army. She was so proud. She encouraged other black men to enlist. In 1863, a large group of black soldiers in Detroit was preparing for battle. Sojourner asked the people of Battle Creek, Michigan, to donate food. She brought the food to the soldiers for a

Thanksgiving dinner. To encourage the young men, she spoke and sang. She wanted to raise their spirits with her words.

Slaves were fleeing from the South and coming to the North. Some joined the army. Others just wanted to make a new life as free men and women. Thousands of these former slaves landed in Washington, DC. They were free now.

But they had no jobs. They had no homes. What would happen to them? Sojourner knew they would need help. She decided to go there and help them.

In 1864, she arrived in Washington. What she saw was terrible. Ex-slaves lived in shacks. They did not have enough food or clothing. They did not know how to take care of themselves because they never had to do it before. But Sojourner had. She would show them all the things they needed to know.

For Aunty
Sojourner Truth
A. Lincoln
Oct 29. 1864

Her work was noticed and praised. She even got to meet President Abraham Lincoln. What an honor! He signed her "Book of Life," a combination autograph book and scrapbook. She was so proud to have his signature in it.

The war raged on for four years. Almost three quarters of a million soldiers lost their lives.

Finally, on April 9, 1865, the Confederate general Robert E. Lee surrendered. The Civil War was over at last. But the South lay in ruins. Houses and property were destroyed. Cities were burned to the ground. It would take years to rebuild.

ROBERT E. LEE

Just a few days after Lee's surrender, President Lincoln went to see a play. While at the theater, he was shot and killed by a pro-Southern actor named John Wilkes Booth. Lincoln's body was laid out in

the East Room of the White House. Thousands of people came to mourn and pay their respects. Sojourner and Sammy were among them.

Vice President Andrew Johnson became the new president. Sojourner met with him. She wanted to talk about the ex-slaves in Washington.

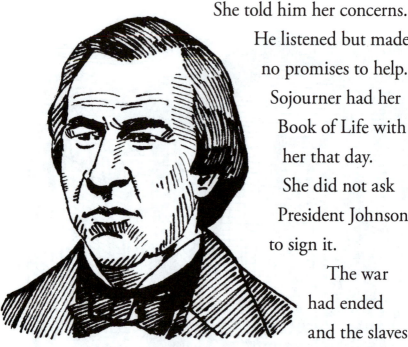

ANDREW JOHNSON

She told him her concerns. He listened but made no promises to help. Sojourner had her Book of Life with her that day. She did not ask President Johnson to sign it.

The war had ended and the slaves were freed. But the newly freed slaves' problems were far from over. And women had not won important freedoms. They still could not vote.

Sojourner was almost seventy years old. She was growing tired. But there was still so much work to do. Sojourner knew she had to keep going.

Chapter 7
A Streetcar Ride

Sojourner continued to help the cause by working for the Freedmen's Hospital. It would be her job to "promote order, cleanliness, industry, and virtue" among the poor blacks who lived there. Being clean was very important to Sojourner. She believed that cleanliness brought a person closer to God.

Many of the former slaves had been field hands. That meant they mostly only knew how to do jobs that they learned while working outdoors on farms. And they had not been paid for their years of backbreaking work. How would they build new lives? They were poor and didn't have the skills needed for jobs offered in the city.

Sojourner thought a lot about this problem. And she was the right person to help solve it.

FREEDMEN'S HOSPITAL

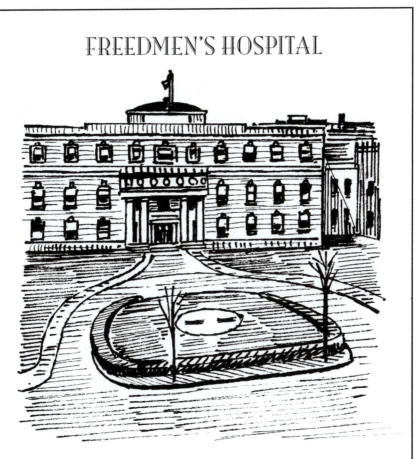

THE FREEDMEN'S HOSPITAL WAS STARTED
IN 1862 TO SERVE THE BLACK COMMUNITY IN
WASHINGTON, DC. IT WAS THE FIRST HOSPITAL
OF ITS KIND TO PROVIDE MEDICAL TREATMENT TO
THE FORMER SLAVES WHO HAD FLOCKED TO THE
NATION'S CAPITAL SEEKING FREEDOM. AFTER THE
CIVIL WAR, THE FREEDMEN'S HOSPITAL BECAME
PART OF HOWARD UNIVERSITY MEDICAL SCHOOL.

Many well-meaning white people could teach skills—like sewing or knitting or cooking—to former slaves. But Sojourner had been a slave. She knew how these people felt. She understood their problems and their pain. She encouraged them to get an education. She also told them they needed to "learn to love white people" who had been working for their cause.

While she worked at the hospital, Sojourner lived in a house at the Freedman's Village. Her grandson Sammy lived there, too. On most days, Sojourner walked to work. At the end of the day, she walked home. But one day she decided to take a streetcar.

She waited at the side of the road.

Two cars passed her. They did not stop. Finally,
she called out in her loud, booming voice. She said
she wanted a ride. The third car stopped for her.
But the conductor was rude and threatening. He
called her names. He made her sit in the back of
the car. That was where black people were forced
to sit. Sojourner did what she was told. But she
was angry.

Another time she wanted to ride a streetcar,

she went with her white friend Laura Haviland. Sojourner tried to get on first. The conductor pushed her aside. He said the white lady should get on first. "I'm a lady, too!" Sojourner said. This made the conductor furious. He shoved her so hard he hurt her shoulder badly.

Sojourner got off the streetcar, but she did not forget about what the conductor had done. She took him to court for hurting her. This was not the first time she had gone to court to accuse a white person. And like the time before, she won. The conductor was fired. After that, other conductors did stop to pick up black people who wanted to ride. Sojourner had won another important battle.

But Sojourner's victory did not last. In time, new laws were passed. These laws kept blacks separated from whites. They could not live or go to school together. They could not eat in the same restaurants. The new laws were known as "Jim

Crow" laws. They stayed in effect in the South for a long time: almost a hundred years.

Sojourner was determined to help former slaves. Around 1867, she got a brilliant idea. The slaves should be paid back for their years of forced labor. But not in money—in land. The government should give free land out West to former slaves. Then they could become farmers. They could use the skills they had. As farmers, they would be productive citizens. They would not need help from anyone.

She was very excited about this idea. Her slogan was "Twenty Acres and a Mule." In 1868, Sojourner's job at the Freedmen's Hospital ended. Now she was able to devote more time to this new cause.

ROSA PARKS, 1913–2005

ROSA PARKS, A BLACK WOMAN, WORKED AS A
SEAMSTRESS AND HOUSEKEEPER IN MONTGOMERY,
ALABAMA. ON DECEMBER 1, 1955, SHE REFUSED TO
GIVE HER SEAT IN THE "COLORED" SECTION OF
A BUS TO A WHITE PASSENGER. THE WHITE
SECTION WAS ALREADY FULL. PARKS'S REFUSAL
SPARKED A LARGE-SCALE BOYCOTT OF THE BUS
COMPANY. THE BOYCOTT MEANT THAT BLACK
CITIZENS OF MONTGOMERY REFUSED TO RIDE
THE PUBLIC BUSES. EVENTUALLY, THE BUS
COMPANY CHANGED ITS POLICY—THOUGH PARKS
LOST HER JOB AND RECEIVED HATE MAIL AND
THREATENING PHONE CALLS. SHE IS NOW
CONSIDERED ONE OF THE HEROES OF THE
MODERN CIVIL RIGHTS MOVEMENT.

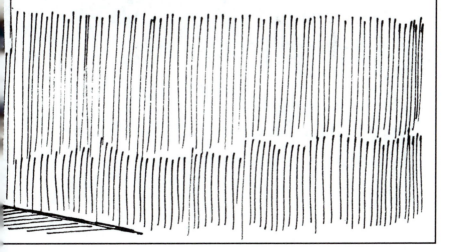

Sojourner and Sammy traveled. She spoke out about equal rights for newly freed blacks. She also continued to speak about women's rights.

Sojourner returned to Washington, DC. On March 31, 1870, she visited President Ulysses S. Grant. He had recently been elected. She wanted his support for her land-grant proposal. The president listened to what she had to say, although their conversation was not written down. However, Sojourner seemed encouraged by his response. She asked him to sign her Book of Life. And when he ran for a second term, she

ULYSSES S. GRANT

supported him. But Grant disappointed her. He did not give her the help she expected.

So Sojourner took her idea to Congress. She
showed up at the Capitol building. In her white
cap, gray dress, and white shawl she looked elegant
and proud. Here is part of what she said
to the senators:

We have been a source of wealth to this
republic. Our labor supplied the country
with cotton . . . and furnished employment

and support for a multitude, thereby becoming a revenue to the government. . . . Our nerves and our sinews, our tears and our blood, have been sacrificed on the altar of this nation's avarice. Our unpaid labor has been a stepping-stone to its financial success. Some of its dividends must surely be ours.

Senator Charles Sumner of Massachusetts was deeply moved by her words. He said he would try to pass a bill if she could prove there was wide support for the plan. Immediately, Sojourner went to work. She had a petition—a document that spelled out what she wanted to get for black people. Underneath was lots of space for signatures.

CHARLES SUMNER

Anyone who signed the petition was agreeing to
her plan. Sammy and another grandson helped.

Sojourner and her grandsons spent eight months
on the road. They went all through New England.
They also went to Delaware, Maryland, New
Jersey, Pennsylvania, New York, Virginia, West
Virginia, and Washington, DC. In each of these
places, she gave speeches and shared her story.

On January 1, 1871, Sojourner spoke to a crowd at Tremont Hall in Boston. She talked about her childhood, the cellar, the beatings, and the pain of being separated from her family. After hearing her, people were eager to sign the petition.

While she was still in Massachusetts, Sojourner heard from her old friend Olive Gilbert. Olive had written down Sojourner's autobiography and was a supporter of women's rights. Now she helped Sojourner get more signatures for the petition.

Sojourner was able to gather thousands of signatures. Now it was time to return to Washington. Surely Senator Sumner would see that there was support for her idea. She had faith in his promise. He would help her.

But when she got there, she learned that the senator had recently died. And so did Sojourner's great idea. No one else believed in it.

The government would not give the support she needed. The former slaves would not get their twenty acres and their mule.

Discouraged and sad, she went back to Michigan. She was tired and she missed home. Also, Sammy was sick. At first his illness did not seem serious. But his fever and cough got worse.

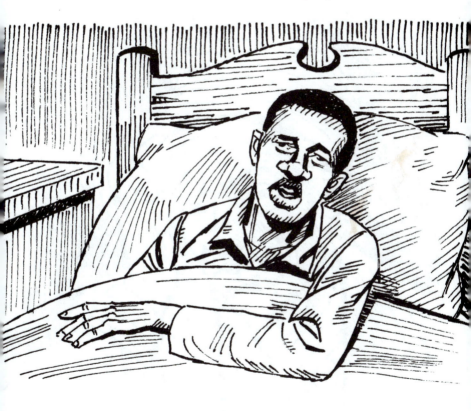

Sammy died in February 1875. He was not even twenty-five years old.

Sojourner missed him terribly. He had been her constant companion. And he had helped her in so many ways. Now she had no one to read to her and no one to write her letters. She felt so bad, she did not want to go on.

Sojourner decided to go home to Battle Creek. She told her family she was going home to die. But Sojourner was wrong. She still had plenty of work to do.

Chapter 8
The Final Years

Sojourner remained committed to the idea of women's rights. She knew Elizabeth Cady Stanton and Susan B. Anthony, two of the movement's most famous leaders. Stanton and Anthony were focused on voting rights.

In order for society to change, women had to be able to vote for new laws. They needed to vote for the leaders they believed in. Without the vote, women had no voice and no power.

Black men had been given the right to vote in 1870. Even so, many Southern states found ways of preventing them from voting. But black women were even worse off. Just as for white women, it was not legal for them to vote.

Sojourner agreed with Stanton and Anthony.

She went to gatherings and gave speeches about women's rights. She said that women would be good leaders, judges, and lawmakers. Often, she was the only black woman at these gatherings. And she was one of the only movement leaders who was poor.

SUSAN BROWNELL ANTHONY
(1820–1906)

SUSAN BROWNELL ANTHONY AND ELIZABETH CADY STANTON WERE TWO OF THE MOST IMPORTANT FIGURES IN THE WOMEN'S RIGHTS MOVEMENT. STANTON WAS A KEY ORGANIZER OF THE SENECA FALLS CONVENTION. SHE AND ANTHONY BEGAN WORKING TOGETHER IN 1851. THEIR GOALS WERE TO ABOLISH SLAVERY AND TO GET EQUAL RIGHTS FOR WOMEN.

ELIZABETH CADY STANTON
(1815–1902)

STANTON ALSO FOCUSED ON GETTING WOMEN EQUAL PAY AND THE RIGHT TO OWN PROPERTY. IN 1872 ANTHONY WAS ARRESTED FOR VOTING IN HER HOMETOWN OF ROCHESTER, NEW YORK. AND IN 1878, ANTHONY AND STANTON PRESENTED CONGRESS WITH AN AMENDMENT GIVING WOMEN THE RIGHT TO VOTE. THEY DID NOT LIVE TO SEE THEIR DREAM COME TRUE, BUT THE NINETEENTH AMENDMENT WAS FINALLY PASSED IN 1920.

Most of the leaders in the women's rights movement had money. They did not have to worry about making a living. They did not need to work at all. Because of this, they did not think about the needs of poor women. Sojourner was different. She had struggled as a black woman. And she had struggled as a poor woman.

She pointed out that men and women were not paid equally for the same work. This made it harder for women to take care of themselves and their families. Sojourner thought that was unfair. She wanted the supporters of women's rights to focus on the issue of equal pay. Until women were *paid* equally, they would not be equal.

Sojourner also believed that women needed to make changes, not just talk about them. She put her beliefs into action. In 1872, she tried to vote in Battle Creek, Michigan. She was turned away. She knew she had to keep fighting. But she did not live to see women get the right to vote.

In 1878, Sojourner went on a speaking tour to thirty-six towns in Michigan. She was eighty-one years old. In that same year, she was also one of three delegates to the Woman's Rights Convention in Rochester, New York. This convention was held on the thirtieth anniversary of the first convention in Seneca Falls.

Some progress had been made since the 1848 convention. In 1851, Amelia Jenks Bloomer started a dress-reform movement for women. Instead of stiff petticoats and uncomfortable long skirts, she urged women to wear loose pants under shorter skirts. This new costume would make it easier for them to get around.

AMELIA JENKS BLOOMER

The pants were named for her: bloomers. In 1869, women began serving on juries in the Wyoming territory. But these were small steps. There was still so much more to be done.

Sojourner could no longer do it. She had spent years fighting for the rights of black people. She had spent years fighting for the rights of women. Now she was old. And tired. She made one last trip to Kansas. She wanted to speak to former slaves who were planning to go out West and farm the land given to them by the government. Then she returned to Battle Creek for good.

Sojourner Truth died on November 26, 1883. She was eighty-six years old. Her funeral was attended by a thousand people. She was buried in Oak Hill Cemetery, near her grandson Sammy. A newspaper in Battle Creek wrote, "This country has lost one of its most important personages."

But Sojourner Truth's bold spirit lives on. Her work and her words continue to inspire and instruct. She was one of America's great heroes, and she will be remembered always.

SOJOURNER TRUTH MEMORIAL
FLORENCE, MA

TIMELINE OF
SOJOURNER TRUTH'S LIFE

c.1797	Isabella born in Ulster County, New York, to Betsey and James
1806	Sold to John Neely
1808	Sold to Martin Schryver
1810	Sold to John Dumont
1815	Falls in love with Robert
1817	Marries Thomas
1818	Birth of first daughter, Diana
1826	Escapes from John Dumont
1828	Moves to New York City with her son, Peter
1843	Changes her name to Sojourner Truth
1850	*The Narrative of Sojourner Truth* is published. Builds a house in Northampton
1851	Gives her famous "Ain't I a Woman?" speech
1857	Moves to Battle Creek, Michigan
1865–1868	Works with the Freedmen's Hospital in Washington, DC
1883	Dies in Michigan on November 26

TIMELINE OF THE WORLD

George Washington is elected first president of the United States French Revolution begins on July 14	1789
Abraham Lincoln is born in Kentucky	1809
Elizabeth Cady Stanton is born in Johnstown, New York	1815
Nat Turner, a Baptist slave preacher, leads a revolt in Southampton County, Virginia	1831
First women's rights convention held in Seneca Falls, New York	1848
Jacob Fussell opens the first commercial ice-cream factory in Baltimore, Maryland	1850
Harriet Beecher Stowe's novel *Uncle Tom's Cabin* is published	1852
Civil War breaks out	1861
Emancipation Proclamation is signed, freeing slaves in the Confederacy	1863
Civil War ends Abraham Lincoln is assassinated in Washington, DC Lewis Carroll publishes *Alice's Adventures in Wonderland*	1865
William Finley Semple patents chewing gum	1869
Thomas Alva Edison develops the first practical incandescent lightbulb	1879
Nineteenth Amendment is ratified; women are given the right to vote	1920

BIBLIOGRAPHY

* McKissack, Patricia C., and Frederick McKissack. **Sojourner Truth: Ain't I a Woman?** Scholastic: New York, 1992.

Painter, Nell Irvin. **Sojourner Truth: A Life, a Symbol**. Norton: New York, 1996.

Truth, Sojourner. **Narrative of Sojourner Truth**. Penguin: New York, 1998. First published 1850.

* Waxman, Laura Hamilton. **Sojourner Truth**. Lerner: Minneapolis, 2008.

* Books for young readers